Ingleborough Cavern and Gaping Gill

by

Trevor D. Ford

DALESMAN BOOKS

1975

The Dalesman Publishing Company Ltd.,
Clapham (via Lancaster), North Yorkshire.
First published 1967 (as "Ingleborough Cavern")
Second edition 1971
Third enlarged edition 1975

ISBN: 0 85206 287 7

The writer would like to thank the following for their assistance in compiling this guide: Mr. R. R. Glover, Mr. B. M. Grainger, Miss Mary Hazleton, Mr. A. Hurworth and Mr. R. Jarman. The survey plan of Ingleborough Cave is based on one by J. Nolan, and that of Gaping Gill on a compilation by John Yeadon of surveys by the University of Leeds Speleological Association, Bradford Pothole Club, Craven Pothole Club, North Ribblesdale Caving Group, Yorkshire Ramblers' Club, Happy Wanderers' Pothole Club and Kendal Caving Club, and also on plans published by Peveril Underground Survey Association and by the Cave Research Group of Great Britain.

Photographs in the text are by the author (pages 18, top; 19, top); Harry Long (page 17); and A. C. Waltham (page 20).

Printed in Great Britain by Galava Printing Company Limited,
Hallam Road, Nelson, Lancashire.

Introduction

ON the south side of Ingleborough lies the picturesque wooded valley of Clapdale, leading down to the village of Clapham. Lying on the A65, the main road from the West Riding to the Lake District and Morecambe Bay, Clapham is easily reached by car or cycle. Frequent bus services from Settle and Skipton to Ingleton, Kirkby Lonsdale, Kendal and Lancaster pass through Clapham.

Ingleborough Cave, or Clapham Cave as it is often known, lies in Clapdale a little over a mile north-east of the village. The dale may be entered by a gate near the timber yard at the top of the village to the left of the waterfall, and a good path leads through the Ingleborough grounds past the lake to the cave. A small charge is made for the use of this path. At least half-an-hour must be allowed for the walk, and if the trees, flowers and birds are to be appreciated, an hour would be more suitable. An alternative route is to take the rough farm road a few yards west of the above-mentioned gate to Clapdale Farm, and to descend into the dale by the farm. The entrance to the cave then lies a few hundred yards up the dale.

Walkers over Ingleborough may approach the cave by passing Gaping Gill and descending the obvious path into Trow Gill and the upper end of Clapdale. In so doing one passes over the inner end of Ingleborough Cave, and over the yet unknown course of the underground river from Gaping Gill.

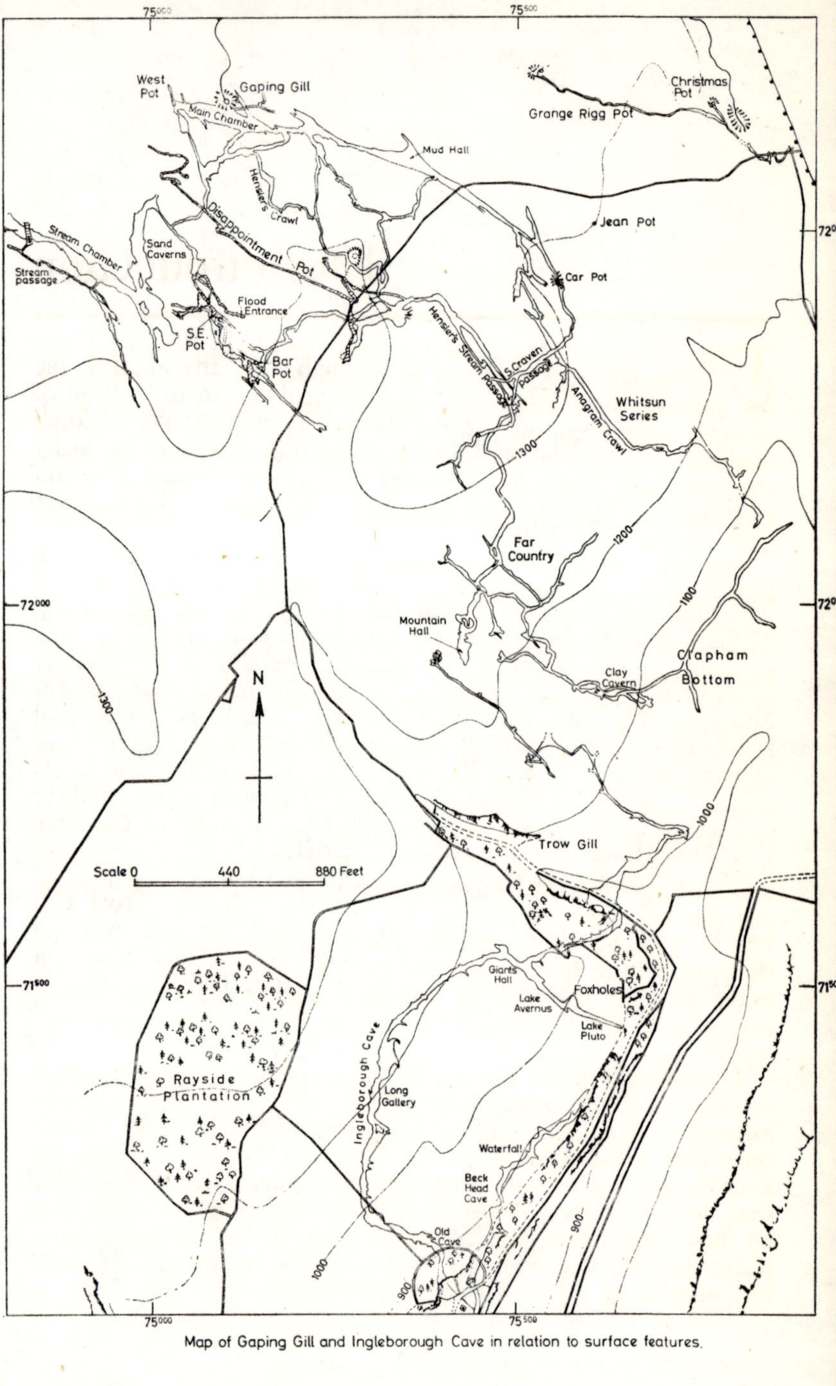

Map of Gaping Gill and Ingleborough Cave in relation to surface features.

Tour of the Cave

THE entrance to the cave is a broad low arch beneath a low limestone cliff overhung by trees. To the right and below the entrance is another cave mouth where the Clapham Beck emerges. More will be said about this cave later, but for the moment it is as well to remember that the Ingleborough Cave was once part of the underground course of the Clapham Beck, and that we shall be walking along the former underground river course.

The cave mouth soon narrows to about eight feet high and wide and a wall and gate have been built across. Around this, deposits of lime known as tufa are to be seen on both sides. After 70 feet we reach the limit of the Old Cave, as it was once known to local inhabitants. At this point a barrier of stalagmite five feet high almost completely closed the passage, and a pool could be seen stretching away into the darkness, at first two feet, and later only 5 inches, from the roof. Following a great flood in Clapdale in 1837, Mr. Farrer, owner of the Ingleborough estates, ordered an excavation where it had burst forth. This was unsuccessful and he then realised that if the barrier was broken down it would release the pool and more cave would become accessible. Mr. Farrer's servant, Josiah Harrison, carried out the task and the cave as we know it today was revealed. The broken ends of the barrier are still visible on either side of the path, and it must be pointed out that in those days it was a brave decision to release an unknown quantity of water from a cave which, for all they knew, might be populated with evil spirits.

Beyond the barrier the pre-1837 water-line is clearly marked at shoulder height along both walls, and various odd stalactite formations hang down to just below the old water-level Among these the most notable is the 'Inverted Forest', a series of knobbly pendant stalactite masses which hang down from the roof, with curious bulbous ends. If 'inverted' to the right way up these would look like miniature trees. In fact, they represent stalactites which grew down to the surface of the ancient pool, but instead of growing further downwards into the water, a different form of lime deposit (tufa) crystallized on them from the pool, giving the knobbly finish.

A little further on, a massive stalactite hangs down with two water-lines on it, indicating former seasonal high and low water-levels. Beyond this old pool cave, the passage rises slightly and expands into Eldon Hall, named after one of Mr. Farrer's friends, Lord Eldon. In here to the right is the massive bank of stalagmite formation, which grew downwards to the old pool level, and which then expanded outwards to give it a mushroom appearance—hence its name, the 'Mushroom Bed'. It has a rippled effect on its surface due to miniature rimstone pools (or micro-gours)—ridges of lime holding back pools with minute crystals of lime in them.

In Eldon Hall is a cluster of the rare twisted stalactite growths known as helictites, in which the power of crystal growth is stronger than the pull of gravity so that the crystals of lime grow sideways and twist upwards like coat-hooks.

Another barrier was found beyond the 'Mushroom Bed' but it was low and a breach on the right was sufficient to drain off the pool, leaving the 'fortification' barrier still lying athwart the rest of the passage. Similar to the mushroom formations there is, some distance ahead, another large stalagmite boss on the left-hand wall. This is the 'Beehive', with its original base corresponding to the former water-level of the second pool, now marked by some five inches long stalactites which have grown in the 130 years since the pool was drained. The walls below the former water-lines are encrusted with the knobbly calcareous pool-deposit, which crystallized from water saturated with lime. This is particularly marked as a band some six inches high at the old water-level, and marks the oscillation from high to low water-level according to the seasons. Close by is the 'Sword of Damocles', a stalactite five feet long.

An impressive cave passage now stretches before us, up to 12 feet high and wide. There are many large pendant stalactites, and before long we can safely cross a bridge over two clear pools of water, into Pillar Hall. Immediately in front is the 'Jockey's Cap', a stalagmite nearly three feet high, and 10 feet in circumference. It has a dimple in the top where drops of water from the roof splash down. Each drop sends a ripple of water down the sides of the Cap so that it is still slowly growing. To the right are the 'Elephant's Legs', a pair of columns five feet high, where stalactites have grown down to meet stalagmites. Opposite is a low bedding cave with numerous thin stalactites which are hollow like drinking straws. Further along the bedding plane a trickle of water emerges to deposit its lime on the 'Rippling Cascade'.

At the far end of Pillar Hall is 'The Pillar', a striking column eight feet seven inches high, from floor to roof. Behind it yawns the 'Abyss', a pit some 20 feet deep with deeply corroded rocks.

It swallows not only the seepage water from this part of the cave, but also the bulk of any flood waters in wet weather. The passage below can be explored for a few yards until roof meets water. The stream reappears at Clapham Beck Head outside the cave entrance.

From Pillar Hall a high and wide passage, 15 to 20 feet high and wide, leads into the 'Curtain Range', passing on our left the the 'Shower Bath', a pair of large stalactites, nearly five feet long, now deeply corroded by an increase in the flow of water down them. Beyond, on the right, are the 'Curtain Stalactites' arranged like clusters of draperies down projections of the limestone wall, in one case to merge with a great stalagmite boss.

The 'Curtain Range' passage illustrates numerous erosional features. The bare limestone is scalloped with concave facets an inch or so across, due to the eddying of turbulent cave streams in the past. The cave widens along the bedding of the limestone strata here, and a bedding plane inlet stream appears from a short branch passage. Unlike the water flowing down the 'Rippling Cascade' this stream is not saturated with lime, and it is still eroding a channel across the floor.

Much of the wall from the 'Curtain Range' onwards is spotted with little white or yellow patches, up to half-an-inch across. Some of the spots are old candle-fat, but most are 'wall-fungus', a primitive and little-understood form of plant life.

As the roof begins to lower, increasing quantities of sand and gravel appear on either side, and in one place on the right their upper surface has been cemented together by stalagmite growth, with the loose material beneath subsequently washed out. The sand beneath has miniature 'lunar' craters in it, where drops of water have fallen persistently in the same spot.

The cave has been comfortable walking so far, but now the roof lowers, though keeping its uniform flatness of the lay of the limestone strata. For a yard or so we have to stoop, and then the roof rises suddenly where a joint or fracture in the limestone crosses the passage. Its cross-section is like a Gothic Arch, and the effect is heightened by draperies of 'curtain stalactites' on each side. Semi-transparent, their folds have multi-coloured effects due to mineral impurities in the lime. Some of the lime deposit is the soft variety known as 'moon milk'.

Behind the curtain stalactites are two stalagmite bosses, which look like pillows, hence the name—'Ladies' Cushions'. But turning to our left along the Gothic Arch passage we enter a new section of cave similar to that we have left. Again there are stalactites and stalagmites on each side—some ring like bells when struck with a key. But one formation is a barrier in miniature, like those which had to be broken to enter the cave, but it is still intact, and holds back a miniature lake. The Long Gallery follows and again displays many features of the complex

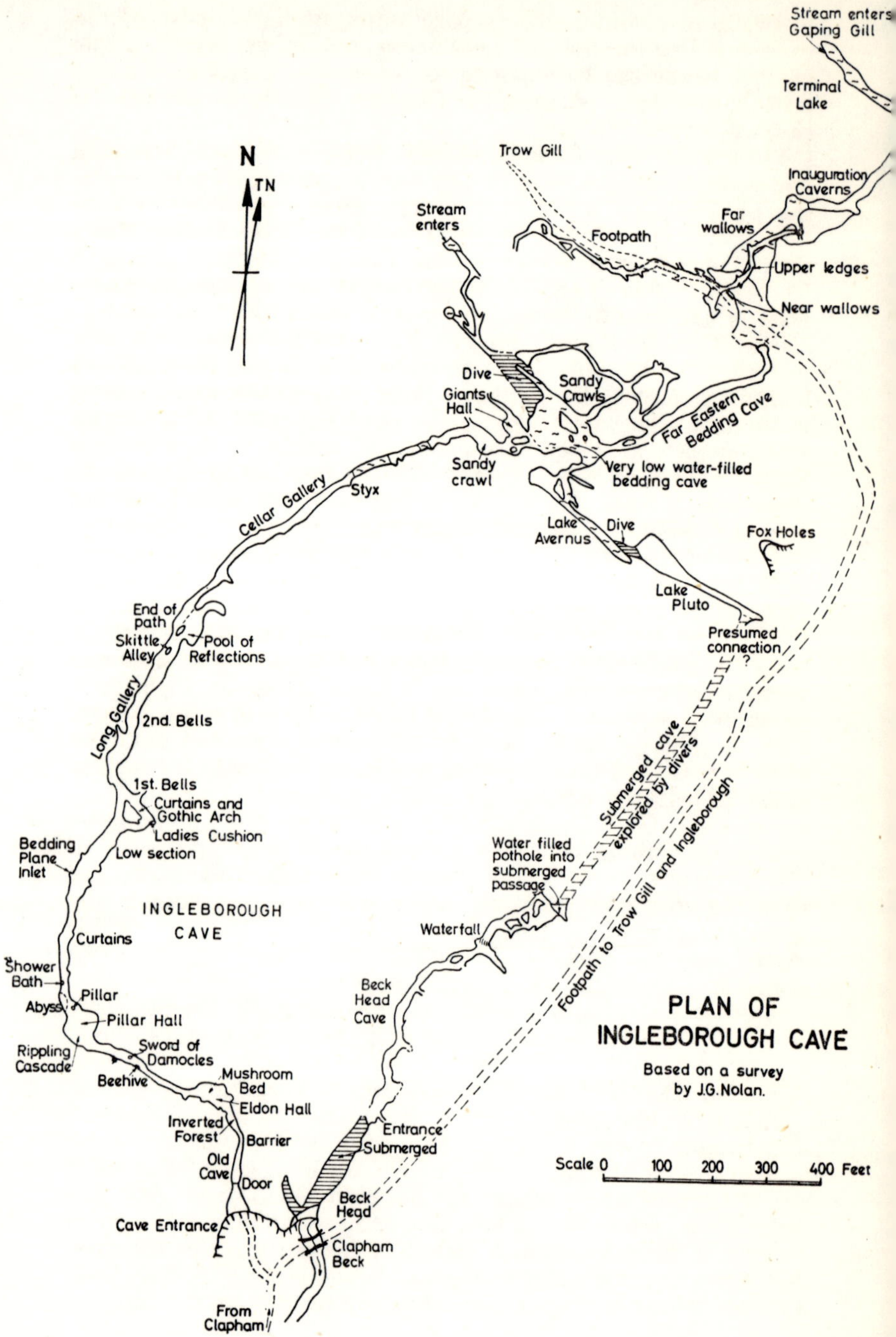

PLAN OF INGLEBOROUGH CAVE

Based on a survey by J.G. Nolan.

history of limestone erosion, and subsequent stalactite growth in this cave. On the right there are patches of an old gravel deposit cemented to the walls by stalagmite, showing that this part of the cave was once full of gravel. Above to the right is the 'Coffee Pot' stalagmite. On the left is another bedding plane inlet with a small stalagmite cascade beneath. A little further on the passage divides for a few yards, our path taking the right-hand branch. The entrance to the left-hand branch has stream-lined scallop facets testifying to the power of the stream which once swept through here.

The thrill of exploring the interior of a mountain is short-lived, however, for the path ends at a point where the cave is no longer 'conditioned' for access of visitors. This point is a quarter-of-a-mile from the entrance. The 'Long Gallery' terminates in a low section with a dark pool, whilst above a shelf on the left the 'Cellar Gallery' beckons the more adventurous. Parties may go beyond to 'Giant's Hall' and 'Lake Avernus', by special arrangement with the management, but there are no footpaths. Instead there are muddy 'wallows', where we get soaked to the skin, and other delights, which may be read about in a later section.

As we turn back an unsuspected branch passage comes into view on the right and a shallow pool reflects the stalactites on the roof in the 'Pool of Reflections'. And we may reflect in another fashion that our tour has taken us a quarter-of-a-mile into the heart of the mountain, without effort or discomfort, along what was once the underground course of the Clapham Beck. In times of heavy flood it still, on rare occasions, becomes an overflow course for the Beck and is washed clean for further generations of visitors.

Exploration in Ingleborough Cave

WHILE the Old Cave, as far as the barrier 70 feet in, must have been known from time immemorial, it was not until 1837 that most of the cave as we know it was first explored. Unfortunately we have no contemporary account in full, but it is known that most of the paths and other improvements had been made by the following year, and that the stream cave below Giant's Hall was reached about that time. Curiously, Giant's Hall itself was not found until a few years later, as its entrance was blocked with a sandbank later removed by flood-waters. By 1852 the cave had been surveyed as far as the stream, and the survey was published by the celebrated Yorkshire geologist, John Phillips, in his **Rivers, Mountains and Sea Coast of Yorkshire.** Thus it was one of the first cave surveys ever published. Ingleborough Cave also has the unique distinction of being the only cave to have its underground course depicted on the Ordnance Survey Maps—and Giant's Hall is named as though it was a topographic feature of the landscape.

Another pioneer geologist, Adam Sedgwick, assisted in the further exploration of the stream cave and has left this graphic account of the low wet passage: "We were forced to use our abdominal muscles as sledges and our mouths as candlesticks". One of the party swam out into what we know now as Lake Avernus, but found no way on.

For many years Lake Avernus was the limit of the known cave, but in the last 20 years or so new exploration techniques have been applied with further successes. In particular, diving with breathing apparatus into completely submerged passages has allowed a few experienced divers to surface in otherwise inaccessible passages. Downstream from Lake Avernus lies Lake Pluto, connected by a low submerged arch, and the water from these reappears in Clapham Beck Head Cave (of which more anon). It should be explained that these 'lakes' are about 100 feet long and up to 10 feet wide and 20 feet deep, mere puddles by surface standards but large enough to be called lakes underground.

Upstream the divers reached a substantial length of open passage only to find another sump at the end, and this has not yet been dived. But it was the 'wallowers' in the low sections below Giant's Hall who had the greatest success. By ploughing through a passage directly beneath the footpath into Trow Gill, barely a foot high and half full of sand and water, they reached a further 500 feet of passages, only to find yet another sump at the end. The Terminal Sump is nearly three-quarters of a mile from the entrance.

The target for cave-divers is Gaping Gill, where water meets roof in Hensler's Passage, little more than a quarter-of-a-mile from the end of Ingleborough Cave. As there is a few feet difference in altitude there must be open passages between, and one wonders if they will ever be explored. Much depends on the cave-diver to pioneer the route. His task is different from most diving since he is unable to surface when in difficulties—there is solid rock in the way. So his equipment and technique must be first class to avoid accidents. A lone diver, Mike Wooding, has recently explored the Terminal Lake; after two submerged sections of passage, each about 300 feet long, he entered a dry passage rising to a high level and extending for a further 800 feet or so. This is believed to be very close to the recently discovered 'Far Country' extensions to Gaping Gill.

Let us suppose that you, reader, are invited to join an exploring party (not a diving party). You change into the oldest clothes you have before entering the cave, for they will be wet through, torn, and covered in mud when you emerge. But make sure they afford protection against the cold—wool next to the skin, thick trousers, strong footwear, a helmet, a good reliable lamp, and a spare means of lighting (candles and matches in a waterproof container). An aqualunger's neoprene rubber wet suit makes a good alternative to the above clothes.

From the end of the path you enter the 'Cellar Gallery', much of it only three to four feet high, where you walk, bent half-double. The first wallows are through the 'Styx', a muddy pool about knee deep, and you wade straight through, making sure you are not the unfortunate one who trips over the submerged boulder halfway, and goes headlong! A little further and a crawl over silt makes you appreciate the value of padding your knees with thick trousers. After a nicely decorated Gothic Arch passage you crawl into Giant's Hall—a misnomer, as it is only about 30 feet long, but a great relief to be able to stand up! Where do we go from here? The route is down an oversize rabbit hole via a muddy chute, where care is needed to avoid landing in the stream at the bottom. The stream cave is wide but low and the way to Lake Avernus necessitates crawling in the stream with barely six inches between roof and water. With the head on one side you can breathe, and you can keep at least part of your body out of the water, but the damp soon seeps upwards. The roof rises and you can walk a few yards to the shore of Lake Avernus—a sheet of water stretching away into the darkness. Close to water-level on the left facing Lake Avernus is the entrance to the Far Eastern Bedding Cave, the route to the Terminal Lake, but this can only be explored by experienced and amphibious cavers. The newcomer to the sport should return before the cold and damp seep in, for the effects of exposure can make themselves felt all too soon.

Clapham Beck Head Cave

IF the cave we have traversed was once a course of Clapham Beck, and is still very rarely occupied by it during flood times, it is reasonable to ask "Where is the Beck's course now?" Part of the answer is obvious for immediately outside Ingleborough Cave is a low cave mouth from which the Beck flows. Unfortunately, only a few yards inside, the roof comes down into the water, and although wide, the passage is too low for even a cave-diver to explore. This mystery of the course of the Beck inside the Beck Head had to wait until only a few years ago for even a partial solution. At a number of points up the dale, narrow clefts in the cliff suggested possible cave mouths concealed by debris fallen from the cliff above.

In 1951 one of these was opened and a cold draught and a murmur of running water could be heard below. Removal of an obstructing boulder allowed entry through an uncomfortable squeeze into a large stream cave—Clapham Beck Head Cave. The entrance is 75 yards up-valley from the Beck Head in the left (west) cliff foot. The passages inside are impressive, up to 12 feet high and wide, leading after 100 yards to a waterfall 14 feet high. But after another 60 yards comes disappointment —the roof comes straight down over where the stream rises from a flooded pothole. The whole cave is only 160 yards of the sought-after underground course. Cave-divers have been down this flooded pothole, 16 feet deep, and explored upstream in a completely submerged passage for nearly 150 yards without finding any way out into open cave passages. At the end they estimated that they were not far from Lake Avernus in Ingleborough Cave. The divers then tried diving downstream from Lake Avernus, and after passing through a low submerged arch they entered another cavern like Avernus, also flooded, which they named Lake Pluto. No way downstream has yet been found, but it cannot be far to the upstream limit of the diver's penetration in the Beck Head Cave.

Gaping Gill Hole

FELL BECK drains the whole southern side of Ingleborough Mountain. With its highest sources at over 2,000 feet above sea level, Fell Beck descends, gathering tributaries, to meet the top of the Great Scar Limestone at about 1,300 feet. The Beck enters a shallow gulley in the boulder clay cover of the limestone plateau and runs for a few hundred yards before plunging into the dark maw of Gaping Gill. Here the funnel-shaped depression in the moor leads into an open shaft, some 20 feet across at the top, where what must be one of the highest waterfalls in Britain plunges 340 feet into the Main Chamber of Gaping Gill.

Long regarded with awe, early attempts to descend Gaping Gill were made by Metcalfe and Birkbeck, though we have little record of their success or otherwise. Birkbeck had a trench cut across the moor to divert Fell Beck; this was reconditioned in 1895 and the Frenchman, E. A. Martel, made the first descent using rope ladders and surveyed the Main Chamber. Many subsequent expeditions have been made and some five miles of passages are now known. There are several 'back-door' entrances which are much less difficult to descend; for example the 'Bar Pot' route requires only two ladder climbs, of 40 feet and 110 feet, and it is dry. In recent years a petrol-driven winch and bosun's chair have been used by caving clubs, and many hundreds have made a safe descent down the enormous shaft and through the roof of the vast Main Chamber.

There is no doubt that the Main Chamber of Gaping Gill is the most impressive cave in Britain. Figures do not do it justice, but for the record it is 500 feet long, 100 feet wide and 110 feet high, similar in size to York Minster! Dim daylight filters down the shaft but does not light the further corners. The diverted Fell Beck appears through a hole in the roof as a waterfall over a hundred feet high, while clouds of spray drift through the gloom. The floor is level but with patches of gravel, sand and mud round the walls, and the stream sinks from view in the gravel patches.

From the Main Chamber there are three main branch cave

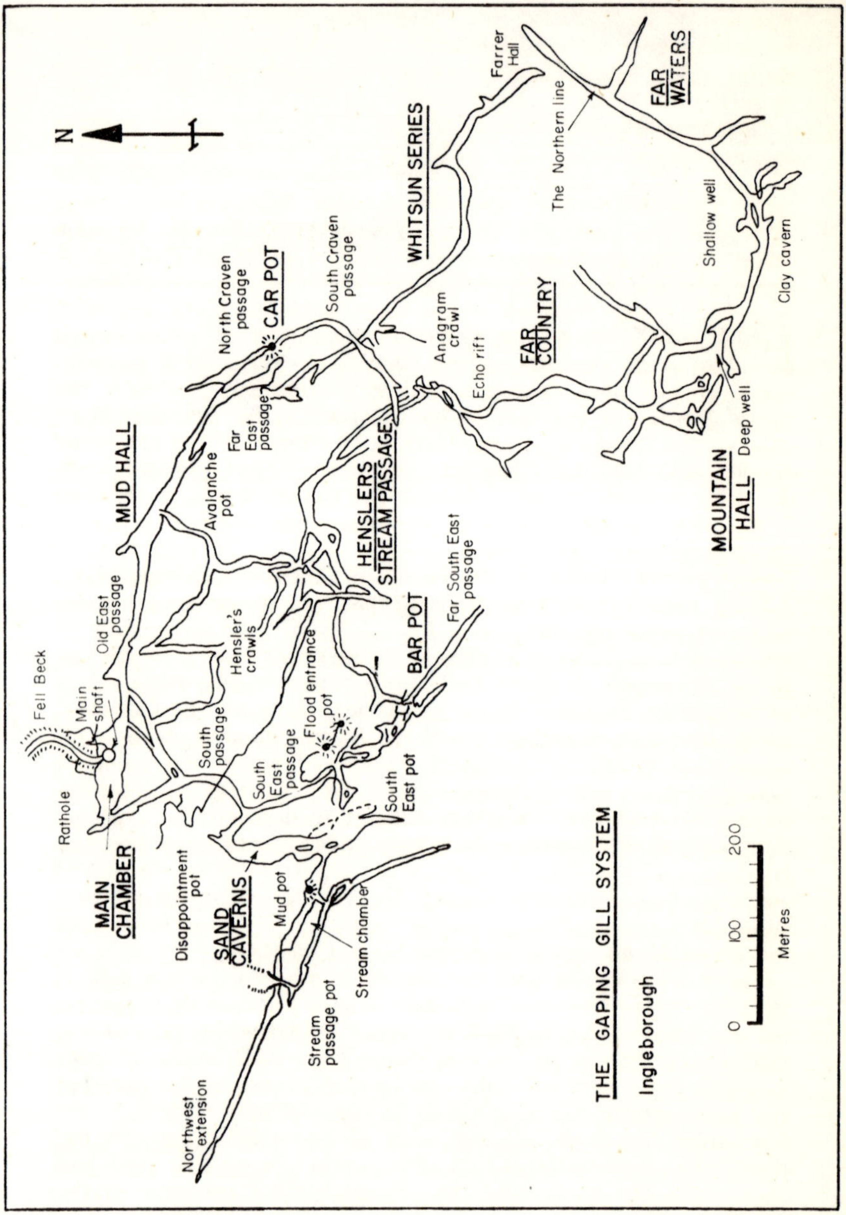
THE GAPING GILL SYSTEM
Ingleborough
0
100
200
Metres
N
MAIN CHAMBER
Rathole
Fell Beck
Main shaft
Old East passage
MUD HALL
Avalanche pot
Henslers crawls
South passage
South East passage
Flood entrance pot
South East pot
Disappointment pot
SAND CAVERNS
Mud pot
Stream chamber
Stream passage pot
Northwest extension
BAR POT
Far South East passage
HENSLERS STREAM PASSAGE
Far East passage
North Craven passage
CAR POT
South Craven passage
WHITSUN SERIES
Farrer Hall
Anagram crawl
Echo rift
FAR COUNTRY
MOUNTAIN HALL
Deep well
Clay cavern
Shallow well
The Northern line
FAR WATERS

systems: west, east and south-east. The west passage system is short and difficult and is much more easily reached via the South-east Passage, so that effectively there are two main branches, with numerous subdivisions. All make a good day's caving sport, and little tackle is needed. Each will be described in turn.

Climbing the east slope of the Main Chamber, a low passage in the right-hand wall is South-east Passage. Of stooping height it soon has a branch on the left leading to the ¼-mile long crawl into Hensler's Passage (see below). Ahead a low section of roof is the Portcullis and crawling under this one can soon stand in the south-western continuation of West Passage. A short way ahead is a T-junction: to the left a crawl over gravel past fine scallop features in the walls leads to South-west Pot. Dropping away 80 feet to the flooded zone, this can be passed by a ledge on the left. Above is a high aven, with passages connecting to Flood Entrance Pot on the surface. Beyond is the large chamber at the foot of Bar Pot, which can be reached by rope ladder climbs from the surface, of 40 and 110 feet. Beyond Bar Pot a stalagmite-cemented heap of large boulders blocks the passage.

Returning to the T-junction and taking the right-hand branch soon leads into Sand Caverns, often used as an underground camp site. The layers of silt and sand at the far end suggest a former intermittent inwashing of detritus from glacier melt-water streams. Climbing over the sandbank one enters 'Stream Chamber, again with many banks of boulders, sand and mud on the floor. A stream enters from the left and can be followed up to where it showers down from a high aven, with linking passages to the surface, rarely used owing to their seeming instability. Banks of stalagmite-cemented gravel rise on each side, and these eventually converge in the North-West extension until a total blockage is reached.

The alternative exploration which can be made from the Main Chamber is along the East Passage, which starts at the top of the East Slope. Now high and dry, this shows evidence of a complex history of development, with at least two phases of inwashing of gravel, cementation by stalagmite and scouring out again. Soon it opens into the vast Mud Hall, not much smaller than the Main Chamber, but with a very uneven floor masking its size. A scramble and then a short ladder climb take one to the bottom. Banks of mud and rocks converge from all sides and the scene is very different from the Main Chamber with the absence of either daylight or running water.

Recently a climb into the roof of Old East Passage, using mountaineering techniques, has revealed a series of chambers rising towards the surface. They reach within 60 or 70 feet of the surface where there is no indication of their presence. As they contain some of the finest stalactite formations in the whole of Gaping Gill it is perhaps as well that they are so difficult of access, or they would doubtless suffer from vandalism.

Scrambling up the slope on the far side of Mud Hall brings one to a concealed crawl under the wall into Hensler's Passage, while Far East Passage continues beyond. This soon splits and not far ahead each of the two branches appears to terminate in small rift chambers. But in recent years each has been the scene of major discoveries. To the left a voice connection may be made with Car Pot, a separate cave system descended via vertical ladder pitches and very narrow crawls from the surface, while just before the end of the south-eastern branch a muddy sump was passed into the Whitsun Series, a complex of muddy crawls and low passages taking one ¼-mile out under the upper end of Clapham Bottoms.

Hensler's Passage may be reached by three routes: it was first discovered in 1937 by Eric Hensler mistaking his route and crawling flat-out through pools of water for ¼-mile. The crawl finally entered a large stream passage with ample room to walk upright. Branch crawls went off in several directions, and following a resurvey a few years ago it was realized that one was close to Mud Hall, and this was soon dug out to make a much easier route into Hensler's Passage. A similar connection was made with Bar Pot chamber, though some crawling is necessary here too. Hensler's stream passage terminated where water met roof, but nearby was a high aven and a number of other small openings. One of these was dug out recently to enter the Far Country, nearly a mile of varied passage with ducks, crawls, walks and a few large chambers, such as Mountain Hall, with an enormous slope of boulders blocking progress. By-passing this, the Far Waters passage requires wading and wallowing, again beneath Clapham Bottoms. Here a crater-like depression on the surface above suggests that a major subsidence has taken place, and it may be responsible for the boulders in Mountain Hall.

One of the avens in Hensler's stream passage has a direct connection with the surface, Disappointment Pot. The open hole on the surface lies only 100 yards south-west of the Main Shaft of Gaping Gill, but exploration terminated in the early days only a short way down where water met roof. A few years ago the intrepid Bob Leakey took a deep breath and plunged through the flooded section, which he luckily found to be quite short. A little digging lowered the water-level and the system lay open for exploration. It was hoped that it would by-pass the end of Hensler's Passage, but once again it was a disappointment as after several ladder pitches it dropped through the roof of the already-known part of 'Hensler's Passage'. Still it provides an exciting through trip to go in via Disappointment and out by one of the other entrances, or vice versa.

One of the ultimate purposes in the exploration of Gaping

The "Inverted Forest", Ingleborough Cave.

"Oxbow Passage", Ingleborough Cave.

Top:— Left: Gravel bank in Stream Passage, Gaping Gill. Right: Solutional features along a bedding plane in Bar Pot. Bottom:— The "Long Gallery", Ingleborough Cave.

Main Chamber, Gaping Gill.

Gill is to follow the course of Fell Beck from where it is last seen sinking in the floor of the Main Chamber to where it reappears in Ingleborough Cave, but so far this has been a vain hope. Tributary streams are seen in various parts of Gaping Gill but the final saturation level is reached only in 'South-east Pot', and this is not on the main flow line. Somewhere beneath the maze of passages which can be explored relatively dry is the active stream cave system, probably completely flooded through much of its length.

Tests to prove the stream connection between Gaping Gill and Ingleborough Cave have been done a number of times. In one test about 1900 half a ton of salt was poured into Fell Beck and detected several days later at Beck Head. Another test with ammonium sulphate in wetter weather still took five days to pass through, though a heavy storm on Ingleborough can displace water at Beck Head within a few hours. More recent tests with dyes such as fluorescein and rhodamine have confirmed that under normal flow conditions the flow-through time from Gaping Gill to Beck Head is between five and fourteen days, but that a flood-pulse can move through the system in under five hours. The distance between Gaping Gill 'Main Chamber' and Beck Head in a straight line is about a mile and the drop is about 480 feet, but between South-east Pot and the Terminal Chamber of Ingleborough Cave is less than ½ mile with very little drop at all, implying that the connecting passage between the two cave systems is largely but not entirely flooded or there would be no five-hour delay in a flood-pulse displacing water at the lower end.

Clearly no opportunity to visit Gaping Gill should be missed. For those who have never done anything of the sort before, the winch and bosun's chair trip into the Main Chamber is an experience which should not be missed. The local caving clubs erect the winch at Whitsun and August Bank holiday weeks only and there are often long queues, but it is worth the wait. For those who want a more extended caving trip, a visit to the system via Bar Pot and its ladder pitches of 40 and 110 feet is the easiest access. But be sure to go with someone who knows what they are doing and uses the proper safety equipment, lifelines and good lights. There are no footpaths, handrails, etc., and even a fall resulting in a sprained ankle can mean a major rescue effort by many people. Joining a well-established caving club is the best way to learn the practice of cave exploration.

The above description of Gaping Gill is only an outline as it is not the purpose of this booklet to provide a comprehensive description and analysis of such a large cave system. While there are numerous articles in caving club journals concerning separate discoveries the only descriptive account which is reasonably complete is in **Yorkshire Caves and Potholes** by A. Mitchell (1949). However, a detailed analysis of the origin and development of the cave system may be found in R. R. Glover's chapter on Gaping Gill in **The Limestones and Caves of North-west England,** compiled and edited by A. C. Waltham (David & Charles 1974).

How Ingleborough Cave was formed

TO understand how any cave is formed one must study the theory of speleogenesis—the theory of cave origin—to appreciate the overall process, and then add to or modify the theoretical picture to account for local details of geological history. So we must start by considering how caves in general are formed, and then apply our ideas to the observed facts in Ingleborough Cave and its surroundings.

In theory, caves may start to form when any mass of limestone rock is uplifted by movements within the earth to a position above sea-level where it is affected by the weather. Any such mass of limestone may have pore-spaces between the constituent grains or it may have joints opened like cracks through the beds, due to stresses caused by the movement. The limestone is usually split into horizontal layers or beds, reflecting former changes in the rate or kind of sediment supplied to the sea floor. The pores, joints and bedding surfaces will be full of water on uplift but provided there is a through route for drainage between interconnected spaces, this 'water-of-sedimentation' will drain away, and will be replaced by rainwater.

Rainwater is weakly acid and slowly attacks limestone, just as hydrochloric acid acts on chalk in a laboratory beaker. But in percolating into the limestone, rainwater picks up humic acids from the decaying organic matter in the soil and these are much more effective in dissolving limestone. One or more of the systems of pores, joints and bedding planes will, by chance, have a greater degree of interconnection and thus less restricted flow-through characteristics; the attack by rainwater and humic acids enhances these and a conduit is formed from the most advantageous route. The further they penetrate into a limestone mass, the more the humic acids are neutralized, but slow solution may take place throughout the conduit system. Such water is discharged at one or more points as springs in the nearest valley. When enlargement of the conduit has proceeded far enough to allow freely flowing streams, the mass of water in the limestone is gradually drained off and streams flow along the

Evolution o

Ingleborough Cav

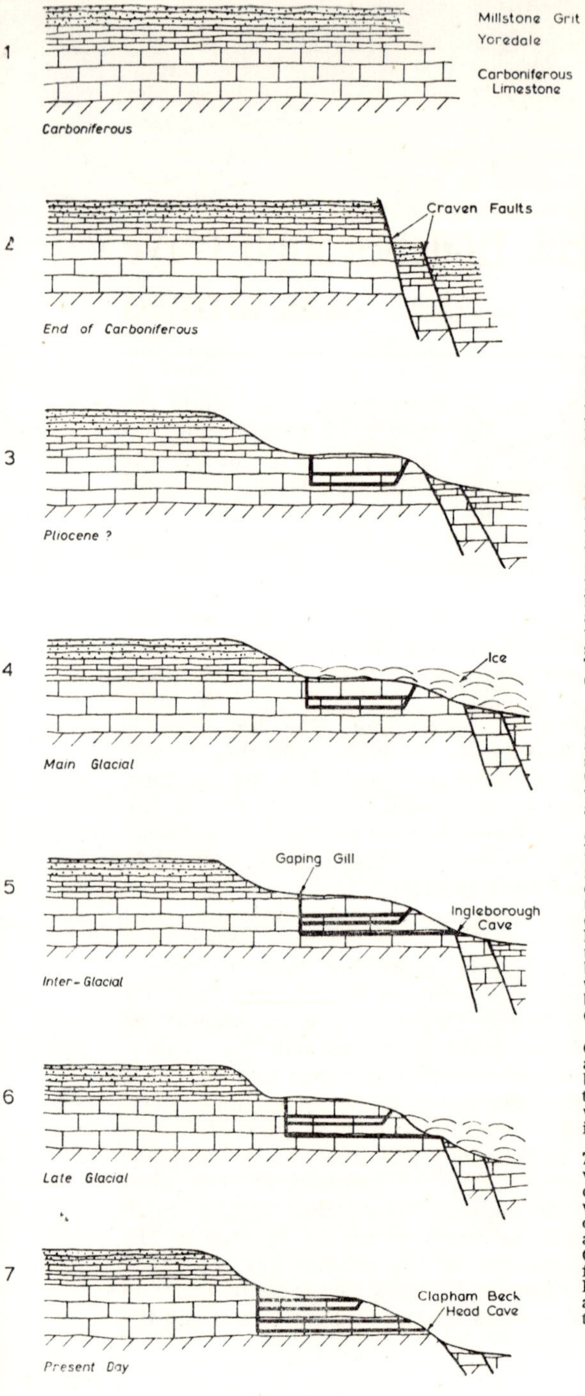

1. The original sediments of the Ca boniferous Limestone, Yoredale Series an Millstone Grit laid down on the sea-floo some 330 million years ago on a surfac of much older slates, steeply inclined.

2. The fracturing of the Earth's crus which produced the Craven faults, starte some 250 million years ago, and cor tinued intermittently up to 30 millio years ago. The faults resulted in down ward displacement of the strata on th south-west side of fractures trending north west to south-east. Parallel fractures wit little or no displacement opened joints i the limestone beds.

3. Erosion of the existing strata was in tiated during the Tertiary era, probabl about 30 million years ago, by the uplift o the Pennine range from beneath the sea In these early stages of erosion Ingle borough was a low hill rising from a plai more or less level with the top of th limestone at 1,400 feet above present sea level. Early rivers eroded shallow valley across the limestone and slow filtration c water took place through the upper beds starting to widen the joints by solution The early stages of the development o Gaping Gill probably date from this phase

4. During the last million years th glaciers of the Pleistocene Ice Ag advanced on and around Ingleborough scouring out the valleys, particularly th Craven Lowlands. The limestone bed were frozen and now underground drain age took place.

5. An Interglacial retreat of the glacier took place, and the ice melted away, leav ing both the valleys and the platea covered with a veneer of boulder-clay— the debris from the melted ice. The re establishment of surface rivers was fol lowed by the progressive loss of water int the limestone down joints, fractures an bedding. Shallow valleys, such as Clapdale were eroded by the surface streams. Ingle borough Cave became the outfall for th Gaping Gill stream.

6. A second but less extensive glacia advance brought glaciers back over Ingle borough once more. The ice scoured ou the valleys but choked the existing cave with debris. Clapdale was probably full o ice.

7. The final melting of the ice allowe vast quantities of melt-water to wash th debris into the caves and to erode thei walls. Surface streams off the higher part of Ingleborough also utilized the caves and the Fell Beck again went down Gaping Gill to emerge from Ingleborough Cav for a time, but subsequently the lowe Beck Head Cave took over the drainag and left Ingleborough Cave dry except i times of flood.

floors of the conduits to the springs, leaving air-filled passages above the water surface. This is the transition from conduit formation below the water table (top of the saturation zone) to conduit enlargement by the erosion of free-flowing streams above the water table, or, as the speleologists (cave scientists) would say, the transition from 'phreatic' to 'vadose' conditions. Seasonal variations in rainfall may cause oscillation in conditions for a time between sub-water-table and free-flow. Only when a conduit becomes large enough to permit the access of Man does it merit the title of **cave.**

During the early stages of this process many small conduits receive the percolating rainfall of a wide area of limestone outcrop, so that little more than pores or open joints appear on the limestone upland surface. Some of these may enlarge by chance roof collapse or by preferential solution to give what are known as potholes or 'sink-holes'. If surface streams flowing from an adjacent area of non-limestone rocks happen to cross on to the limestone, they may at first leak into the initial limestone conduits, and then enlarge these so that the whole stream goes underground to join the limestone drainage. The preferential enlargement of such a 'boosted' system of conduits forms a cave system much more quickly at the expense of its neighbours which then become tributaries.

The boosted stream may carry along sand and boulders, particularly in time of flood, and the turbulent flow causes the sand-laden water to scour out the scallops or facets so common in stream caves, thus enhancing features produced by the corrosion of limestone by solution in percolating rainwater.

The progressive erosion of the valley in which the springs discharge may mean that new lower conduits come into operation with the eventual abandonment of the higher channels, leaving dry former caves of debouchure, and dry upper galleries in the caves within.

On turning to Ingleborough this sequence of events can be followed without difficulty but there have been a number of modifying factors. Ingleborough Cave is in the Carboniferous Limestone, i.e. a limestone sediment made up of finely fragmented shell debris on the sea floor of the Carboniferous period of geological time, roughly 330 million years ago. Subsequent to its formation the Carboniferous Limestone was buried under thousands of feet of other sediments, notably the shales and sandstones of the Yoredale Beds and Millstone Grit, which still form the upper part of Ingleborough mountain. Burial such as this affects the pore-spaces between shell fragments and effectively the whole pore-space of the limestones of Ingleborough was filled in by a natural cementation process. Exceptions are adjacent to some shale-bands along the bedding surfaces.

Following deep burial there were more earth movements

resulting in great earthquakes, one series of which formed the Craven faults, which today form the southern boundary to the limestone mass of Ingleborough. Secondary stresses set up by the earthquakes opened a strong set of north-westerly trending fractures now seen as joints, which have controlled the direction of formation of many of the passages in Gaping Gill and Ingleborough Cave, e.g. Gothic Arch Passage, Lakes Avernus and Pluto, also the 'Waterfall' and the 'Sump' in the Beck Head Cave.

The main uplift of the Pennine mountain range from far below sea-level is believed by geologists to have occurred during the Tertiary period of geological time, about 30 million years ago. Much of the period since the uplift was occupied by erosive forces of wind and weather stripping off the cover of Yoredale Shales, Millstone Grit and younger strata, and we have little evidence of the details of this stage or its results.

Most of our story is concerned with the events of the last one million years, known to geologists as the Pleistocene period, during which occurred the Great Ice Age. In this, glaciers advanced from the Scottish Highlands and Scandinavia three and probably four times over the Pennines, and between the advances melted away again. Almost the whole of our scenery in the Ingleborough region is due to this alternation of glacier movement—scouring away loose rock here and dumping it as boulder-clay elsewhere—and inter-glacial periods of temperate climate with normal river erosion. Much of the story is still unknown and controversial to geologists, so that only a generalised account can be told here.

At the beginning of the Pleistocene period Ingleborough mountain seems to have been a much wider hill with fairly gentle slopes rising from a landscape generally level with or not far below the edge of the present limestone plateau. The whole limestone mass was below the water table and deep water-flow opened out many of the north-westerly joints and some bedding planes during the early phreatic development stage. As the sea-level fell so the rivers draining the Pennines adjusted to progressively lower outfalls by eroding their beds, and thus deepening their valleys. This allowed the beginnings of drainage of the upper parts of the limestone and the initiation of some of the high level cave passages. Other high level passages developed progressively as more and more of the limestone became freely drained. At this stage Ingleborough Cave was mostly submerged joint and bedding cave passages.

During the Pleistocene period was the Great Ice Age, and glaciers advanced from the Scottish Highlands, Lake District and North Pennines over the Ingleborough region. Each advance saw a phase of active ice during which scouring of both the upland surface and the existing valley floors took place, and a phase of stagnant ice when the effect of melting was to deposit as boulder-clay, the material scoured from further north. Each phase of scouring on Ingleborough removed part of the cover of Yoredale Shales and Millstone Grit to expose more limestone. It also allowed some deepening of the valleys so that lower levels of the limestone's initial drainage became active; this is reflected in scattered high level passages in some caves though little has been found in appropriate positions in Gaping Gill or Ingleborough Cave.

The greatest effects of the Ice Age are those of the penultimate advance of glaciers over Ingleborough, some 250,000-150,000 years ago. All loose soil from the Ingleborough plateau was removed; part of the remaining cap of Yoredale Shales and Millstone Grit was removed to expose more limestone; most existing cave entrances were blocked with debris, and those that were not blocked became choked with ice so that summer melt-water streams from the glaciers had to flow over the ground or ice surface; boulder-clay was brought in from further north and 'dumped' on Ingleborough. Also during this phase Chapel-le-Dale, Ribblesdale, and the valleys to the south were excavated to approximately their present depth.

But what about Clapdale and Ingleborough Cave? At this early stage of glaciation it can be argued that at first the dale was very much shallower than at present; that the present stream course through the Beck Head Cave was probably no more than a hair crack between limestone beds; that Ingleborough Cave itself was a phreatic cave of joints and bedding being opened out further by more solution. During and after the melting of the glaciers in the Last Interglacial phase (150,000-40,000 years ago) still more solutional and, later on, abrasional development took place. At first the ground was frozen and the drainage of melt-water was over the surface, cutting out the gorge of Trow Gill along one of the north-westerly joints, and deepening Clapdale to its present form. As the ground thawed so drainage utilized the joints and bedding already slightly opened by solution. As more ice melted on the plateau above, its melt-water escaped into the underground drainage, particularly via the large solution-cum-collapse cavity of Gaping Gill. Until Clapdale was deepened far enough for the Beck Head cave passages to become the channel, Ingleborough Cave was the active stream cave and was enlarged by the erosion of melt-water streams to its present size.

Ingleborough Cave must thus be regarded as the chief drainage route for the waters once released by the melting of the glaciers and sheets of ice covering Ingleborough, but it has subsequently lost its drainage to the Beck Head Cave. During the final advance of the ice in the last Glacial episode between 40,000 and 10,000 years ago, much of the above sequence was repeated, with the difference that Clapdale was partly refilled with boulder-clay, blocking the former outflow cave at Foxholes. The orifice of Gaping Gill itself was covered in boulder-clay which has since collapsed into the shaft below. Probably many of the passages of both Gaping Gill and Ingleborough Cave were filled with inwashed sediments when the outfall became blocked by ice. The retreat of these ice sheets, some 10,000-15,000 years ago, allowed the melt-water to clear out much of the boulder-clay from Clapdale, and to remove much of the sediment from Ingleborough Cave, leaving only a few passages choked with sand, though a lot of silt remains in the passages of Gaping Gill.

The Last Glacial phase also saw the erosion of the country south of the Craven faults to a lower level, so that the streams such as Clapham Beck have since started to erode their beds down to that level. The steepened new course of Clapham Beck is now largely masked by the artificial dam in the wood above the village, but the gorge-like section between the dam and the open part of Clapdale below the farm is evidence of this erosion. In this gorge Clapham Beck has eroded through the bottom of the Carboniferous Limestone into the underlying impervious slates, and springs may be found in Clapdale woods emerging along the contour of this junction between two rocks. This junction lies about 100 feet below the floor of Ingleborough Cave and it will be, sometime in the distant future, the final limit of downward penetration of the underground drainage. As yet it has had little effect on the form of the cave system, unlike White Scar Cave where the roof of the entrance passage is in limestone but the floor is slate.

The question is often asked by visitors "How old is Ingleborough Cave"? From the above it can be deduced that:

a) The limestones enclosing the cave are of Carboniferous Age, i.e. about 330 million years old.

b) The formation of the joint system through the limestones date from successive earth movements between 250 and 30 million years ago.

c) The gradual opening of the joints and bedding by slow, deep solution took place largely during the latter part of the Tertiary era, during the last 30 million years.

d) The main phases of development of both Gaping Gill and Ingleborough Cave seem to have taken place during and between the main ice advances of the Pleistocene period of geological time, i.e. between 250,000 and 10,000 years ago. Varying amounts of water under differing climatic conditions enlarged the primary conduits and transported vast amounts of sediment into the system, some of it being washed out by floods today. Clapdale was progressively deepened during these phases by ice scour, by the rapid run-off of melt-water from the glaciers and by the freeze-and-thaw fracturing of the rock during waxing and waning stages of glaciation. It is still being deepened by the erosion of the Beck.

(e) Stalactite formations in the caves are thus either relics of deposits formed during the warmer climatic phase of the Last Inter-glacial period (150,000-40,000 years ago) or they have been formed since the Last Glaciation, in the last 10,000 years. Most date from this last episode.

Stalagmites and Stalactites

ONCE a cave has been formed and drained to such an extent that its roof is no longer submerged, percolating rainwater from the surface may soak through and drip from the roof to form stalactites. Rainwater is slightly acid, owing to its content of carbon dioxide dissolved from the atmosphere; it easily becomes more acid on passing through soil, with decaying vegetable matter yielding humic acids. Acid waters attack the limestone through which they percolate, taking limestone into solution as calcium bicarbonate. On emerging from a pore-channel through a cave roof one or more of several things may happen:

1) Some of the excess carbon dioxide obtained from the neutralization of humic acids may be discharged in the cave air, thus causing at least some of the remaining calcium carbonate to crystallize around the point of emergence. If the flow is relatively fast the rest of the drop of water falls away to the floor leaving only a minute ring of calcium carbonate; one ring on another builds a hollow tube-shaped 'straw' stalactite. If the flow is relatively slow a platelet or calcium carbonate is left, and one platelet on another builds up a rod stalactite.

2) Some of the percolating water may evaporate, thus both discharging carbon dioxide and precipitating calcium carbonate. Evaporation normally only takes place if the temperature and humidity of the cave air are markedly different from normal cave air (48°F and 98% humidity) or where there are strong draughts (usually near entrances). The lime so deposited is usually knobbly and porous and does not form good straw or rod stalactites.

3) Airborne bacteria in the cave may utilize some of the carbon dioxide in solution in the percolating drops of water, thereby causing a biochemical precipitation of calcium carbonate,

usually in a very finely divided form known as 'moon milk'. These are usually most common near entrances or where there are strong draughts.

In many cases two, or all three, of these processes take place at the same time, the last two being particularly effective in cave entrances, where the rough knobbly calcium carbonate deposits are usually known as 'tufa'. Warm springs often produce much the same material, also by bacterial and evaporative action.

Ingleborough Cave contains good examples of all three forms of stalactite. The entrance passages are encrusted with much tufa, while the inner part of the cave has numerous straw and rod stalactites formed by the first process. The barriers at the end of the old (pre-1837) cave are of tufa built up by the precipitation of lime by bacterial action and evaporation where lime-rich seepage waters discharged over a gentle rock ridge, long since obscured. Some of the larger formations further in, such as the 'Shower Bath', appear to show some influence of the latter cause of deposition as well as the more normal carbon dioxide discharge of the first type. The 'Inverted Forest' is a group of large tufa stalactites which grew downwards, and then gained 'foliage' from tufa deposited on these stalactites during periods when the pool behind the barrier was low.

The normal rod and straw stalactites often have stalagmites beneath, owing to the falling excess water discharging its carbon dioxide when it lands. Discharge of carbon dioxide means precipitation of lime, which builds up as a stalagmite. If stalactite and stalagmite meet they form a column. If the drips of water tend to run down the edge of an overhanging rock they form a stalactite curtain, often with a serrated edge.

Many of the stalagmites, particularly 'Mushroom Bed', show a rippled effect with minute hollows lined with calcite crystals behind each ripple. These are micro-gours, to use the French term, and are caused by the discharge of carbon dioxide over an irregularity, precipitating a build-up of lime on the edge of the ripple. It may build up a series of terraced pools.

Calculations of the age of a cave are often made on the basis of the rate of growth of a single stalactite or stalagmite during the last century at most. Such a concept is false. There are too many variable factors affecting stalactite growth. The first is that the climate, and hence rainfall. have varied considerably since the end of the Ice Age, some 10,000 years ago, so that the rate of percolation into the limestone has varied. Secondly, the amount and nature of the vegetation cover has varied since the Ice Age and is by no means constant over a whole limestone area. Thirdly, the pattern of joints and bedding providing seepage routes is highly varied. Fourthly, the temperature and humidity in the cave passages have varied since the Ice Age, and still do slightly. These, and other factors, mean that no two stalactites are likely to have had the same growth history; and no two are still growing at exactly the same rate. Even so, the stalactites of one section of a cave are likely to have had some similarities in their growth histories, so that if measurement can be taken of several and averaged it will give us some idea of the rate of growth today, though not necessarily far into the past. No such measurements have been taken, as yet.

All we can say is that as far as the geological evidence goes almost all the stalactite formations in Ingleborough Cave are younger than 20,000 years, probably less than 10,000 years. Some stalactites started growth early and grew fast so that they are several feet long, while others started late and grew slowly so that they are but an inch or so long. Growth rates thus vary from perhaps an inch per century down to an inch in 5,000 years. Growth rates on stalagmites are similarly highly varied, and much the same figures apply. The tufa near the cave entrance may grow much faster under favourable conditions; an inch in 10 years is possible but no measurements have been taken in Ingleborough Cave.

Some of the earliest known attempts to measure the rate of growth of a stalagmite anywhere in the world were made on the Jockey Cap stalagmite. Unfortunately the measurements have been taken in different places by different investigators and the results are therefore not very reliable. Some measured the circumference at the base but this undulates so it is not clear where one should measure it today for comparison; others measured the slope height from the base to the apex, again without being clear as to the exact positions of the points of reference. Still others measured from the roof to the apex, and the stalactite directly over the Jockey Cap was broken off during one set of measurements in 1853! Professor Boyd Dawkins drilled holes in the base and inserted wooden plugs in 1873, but these could not be found recently. In 1904 Hill thought there had been a decrease in the rate of growth, and this seems to have some support from measurements made in 1967, which showed that it had grown no more than ½-inch in 63 years. The figures have often been quoted and may be summarized thus:

Year	Circumference at base	Growth
1839	118 in.	
1845	120 in.	1 in. per 3 years
1873	128 in.	1 in. per 3·5 years
1892	128 in.	nil
1904	128 in.	nil

Year	Height from crown to roof	Growth
1845	95¼ in.	
1873	87 in.	1 in. per 3·5 years
1892	86 in.	1/20 in. per annum
1904	86 in.	nil

Measurements in 1967 suggest that it had grown only ½-inch higher in the last 63 years, and the girth has not substantially changed.

On the basis of some of the early figures, the Jockey Cap is no more than 400 or 500 years old, but this is quite inconsistent with the geological evidence, which suggests that an age approaching 10,000 years would be more reasonable. In fact, all that the figures do (if we accept them as correctly measured) is to show that the rate of growth has varied over the centuries. To support this deduction we may note that Dr. Pitty, then at Oxford University, took detailed measurements of the rate of drip and of the amount of calcium carbonate in the drops, and found that both these varied considerably according to the amount of rainfall during the preceding weeks.

Ingleborough Cave and Prehistoric Man

OUR prehistoric ancestors frequently inhabited caves, sometimes as a permanent dwelling place, sometimes as a temporary shelter while out hunting, and sometimes as a refuge while being hunted! An open cave mouth such as Ingleborough Cave must have attracted their attention, but no remains of prehistoric occupation have ever been found in the cave. The reasons are fairly obvious: the occasional floods would have prevented permanent use and the barrier at the end of the Old Cave would have made use as a refuge unlikely as there would be nowhere to hide. Occasional visits by these hunters would leave little debris, and that would soon be washed away.

By contrast, Fox Holes, some 400 yards further up Clapdale beneath the cliff on the west side, has yielded remains of occupation. During excavations in 1913-14 in what appears to have been an old overflow passage from the Gaping Gill-Ingleborough Cave drainage blocked with boulder-clay, a crude stone wall was found, buried in scree fallen from the cliff above, and behind it were a number of stone implements of late Neolithic type, say, 1500-2000 B.C., as well as bones of various animals, including wild ox, Irish elk and red deer. A few fragments of Neolithic pottery were found, as well as a few human bones, suggesting that the cave had been used for burial as well as temporary habitation. The outbreak of the 1914 war prevented completion of the dig, which only penetrated 20 feet inwards, and further investigation is still needed. The bones have been preserved in the British and Manchester Museums.

Life in Ingleborough Cave

Most people think of caves as being completely devoid of life, but this is far from the truth. Many caves contain a wide range of living species, either from choice or by accident. Some of these species have been washed in by flood waters, or are descended from such accidental arrivals. Others have flown in for winter hibernation and have stayed put, while still others are species which live almost exclusively in caves and crevices.

Any form of animal life requires food, either another animal or a plant, and complete chains of species, feeding on each other may be found in caves. At the beginning of the chains there may be either or both of two starting points—organic debris washed in from the surface, or bacteria which derive their nourishment from the environment's inorganic materials, salts in solution in water, gases in the air such as carbon dioxide, etc., and traces of carbon, sulphur or iron compounds in the rock.

No systematic study of Ingleborough Cave's biology has been done, but a substantial list of species has been compiled. The most lowly form of life appears to be the 'wall-fungus' of the Curtain Range and Long Gallery. This is probably an intergrowth of filamentous bacteria known as *Streptomyces* and lowly fungi such as *Fusarium*. Other species may be present.

The streams and pools contain the common freshwater shrimp, *Rivulogammarus pulex,* often showing loss of pigmentation. These feed on the Cyclopoids also found in the streams. Near the pools, springtails may be found under stones or in crevices in the walls. Various flies and beetles have been found and include scavengers feeding on plant debris washed in during floods and on wall-fungus, as well as predators feeding on springtails and flies. Occasional spiders and mites also feed on the flies and springtails. Rare bats take up a temporary residence, and pale trout have been seen near Lake Avernus.

List of species recorded in Ingleborough Cave
(In the records of the Cave Research Group of Great Britain)

ANNELIDA OLIGOCHAETA	*Allolobophora? chlorotica* (Savigny)
ARTHROPODA	
DIPLOPODA CHORDEUMIDA	*Polymicrodon polydesmoides* (Leach)
INSECTA COLLEMBOLA	*Onychiurus fimitarius* group *Onychiurus schoetti* (Lie-Petterson) *Folsomia candida* (Willem) *Folsomia quadrioculata* (Tullberg) *Isotoma* (*Vertagopus*) *arborea* (Linne)
EPHEMEROPTERA?	*Ecdyonurus venosus* (F.) larva
COLEOPTERA	*Ancryophorus aureus* (Fauvel)
TRICHOPTERA	*Plectrocnemia conspersa* (Curtis)
DIPTERA	*Bradysia* sp.
CRUSTACEA CYCLOPOIDA	*Acanthocyclops viridis* (Jurdine)
AMPHIPODA	*Rivulogammarus pulex* (Linne)
ARACHNIDA ACARI	*Eugamasus magnus* (Kramer) *Rhagidia ferricola* (Koch)

The cover photographs show:- Front: "The Crystal Pool" below the clear surface of whi ... bly calcareous deposits from ... **H. Metcalfe).** Inside back, to ... the "Beehive" **(M. H. Long** ... h" **(Nicholas Barrington).** Al ... of large stalactites nearly five

9780852062876